INSIDE THE
SUN

Harold G. Kelly

The Rosen Publishing Group's
READING ROOM
Collection

New York

Published in 2002 by The Rosen Publishing Group, Inc.
29 East 21st Street, New York, NY 10010

Copyright © 2002 by The Rosen Publishing Group, Inc.

First Library Edition 2002

Book Design: Haley Wilson

Photo Credits: Cover, pp. 1, 4, 8, 11, 15, 16 © Digital Vision; p. 6 © Mike Aglolo/International Stock; p. 12 © Guy Motil/Corbis; p. 19 © Telegraph Colour Library/FPG International; p. 20 © Patrick W. Stoll/Corbis; p. 22 © Warren Morgan/Corbis.

Kelly, Harold G. (Harold Greg), 1968-
        Inside the sun / Harold G. Kelly.
                p. cm. -- (The Rosen Publishing Group's reading
        room collection)
        Includes index.
        Summary: This book discusses the formation of the sun
and the planets and explains how the sun gives heat, light, and
energy to living things.
        ISBN 0-8239-3730-5
        1. Sun--Juvenile literature   [1. Sun]   I. Title
II. Series
        QB521.5 K44   2001-006832
        523.7--dc21

Manufactured in the United States of America

For More Information
Starchild: The Sun
http://starchild.gsfc.nasa.gov/docs/StarChild/solar_system_level2/sun.html

Contents

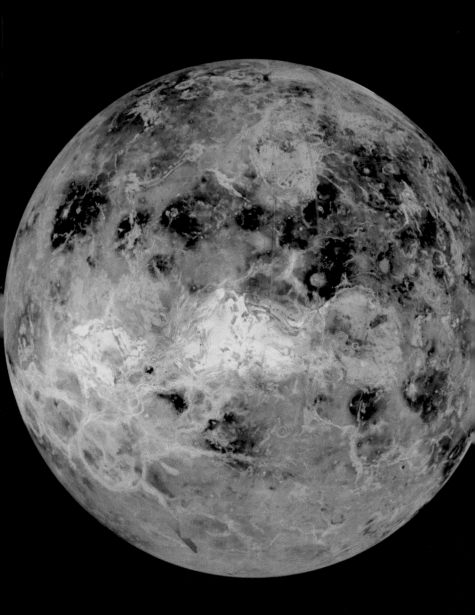

How the Sun Was Formed

The sun is very important to us. There could be no life on Earth without the sun's light and heat. It may seem to us that the sun has been around forever, but it hasn't. A long time ago, our sun didn't exist. Most **astronomers** believe the sun was formed about 4.5 billion years ago. That may sound like a long time, but to scientists who study space it's really a short amount of time!

The sun is a very large, glowing ball of gases in the middle of our **solar system**. Earth, eight other planets, and their moons travel around the sun. Long ago, the sun was just a huge cloud of gas and dust, and our solar system did not exist.

The sun is the center of our solar system. Earth and eight other planets move around the sun.

Scientists believe that about 4.5 billion years ago, some of this gas and dust began to fall in on itself. This produced a lot of heat. The gas and dust began to shine. This is how the sun was formed. After the sun formed, the gas and dust that were left over began to travel around the sun. This gas and dust formed the moons and the nine planets of our solar system.

The nine planets in our solar system are Mercury, Venus, Earth, Mars, Jupiter, Saturn, Uranus, Neptune, and Pluto. The planet that is closest to the sun is Mercury. The planet that is farthest from the sun is Pluto. The sun is about 100 times larger than all of the planets put together!

Our sun, the planets and moons of our solar system, and even Saturn's rings were made from gas and dust.

Our Sun the Star

The sun is a star, just like all the twinkling stars you see in the night sky. The reason our sun looks so different from other stars is because it is the closest star to us, even though it is more than 92 million miles from Earth! The sun is just one of the billions of stars in our **galaxy**, which is called the Milky Way. Our galaxy is called the Milky Way because on clear nights, it looks like a milky band of light in the sky.

The stars in the Milky Way fan out in a **spiral** shape from the center of the galaxy. Our solar system is just a tiny part of the Milky Way. It is located on one of the galaxy's long, curving arms.

There are over 100 billion stars in our galaxy, the Milky Way.

The sun is made of many different kinds gases. About three quarters of the sun is mac up of **hydrogen** gas. Hydrogen is a very light gas that burns easily. Almost one quarter of the sun is made up of **helium** and very small amounts of at least seventy other kinds of gases. Like hydrogen, helium is also a very ligh gas, but it does not burn the way hydrogen does. Because the sun is made only of gases, something is needed to keep all of the gases together. **Pressure** does this important job.

Pressure is the force that one thing puts on another. Pressure happens when somethin pushes against something else. The pressure, or force, pulling the gases toward the center of the sun is the same as the pressure pushing the gases away from the center of the sun. This pressure is what makes the sun's gases stay together.

The sun might look like a solid ball to us, but it is really made of gases that are held together by pressure.

11

The sun's center is called the core. The **temperature** in the sun's core is about 27 million degrees. This is the hottest part of the sun. The sun gets its energy from the hydrogen in its core. There is a lot of pressure on the sun's core. This pressure changes the hydrogen gas into helium gas. Energy is released when helium is created. The sun needs energy so it can keep shining as a star.

It takes hundreds of thousands of years for energy from the core to reach the surface of the sun. When this energy gets to the surface, sunlight is released. It takes only about eight minutes for sunlight to reach Earth. This is because light travels very fast.

The hydrogen in the sun's core is what gives the sun its energy.

The Part of the Sun We Can See

The sunlight that we see is from the layer of the sun called the **photosphere**, or light sphere. The photosphere is about 125 miles thick. The energy that is released from the photosphere has made a very long journey from the sun's core to the sun's surface. The average temperature of the photosphere is about 6,000 degrees.

The photosphere has dark spots on it called sunspots. Sunspots are darker because they are cooler than the rest of the photosphere. A sunspot only lasts for a few weeks. An early astronomer named Galileo (gal-uh-LAY-oh) noticed that sunspots are always moving, and he realized that the sun spins on its own **axis**.

The temperature of sunspots can be thousands of degrees cooler than the rest of the sun's photosphere.

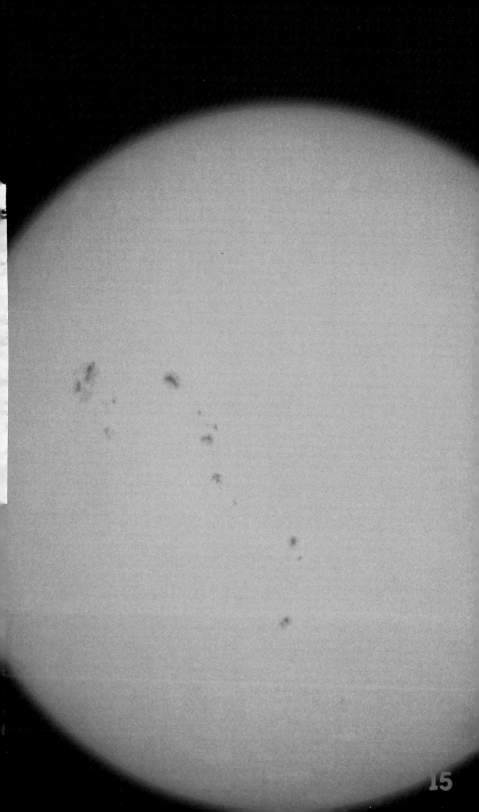

15

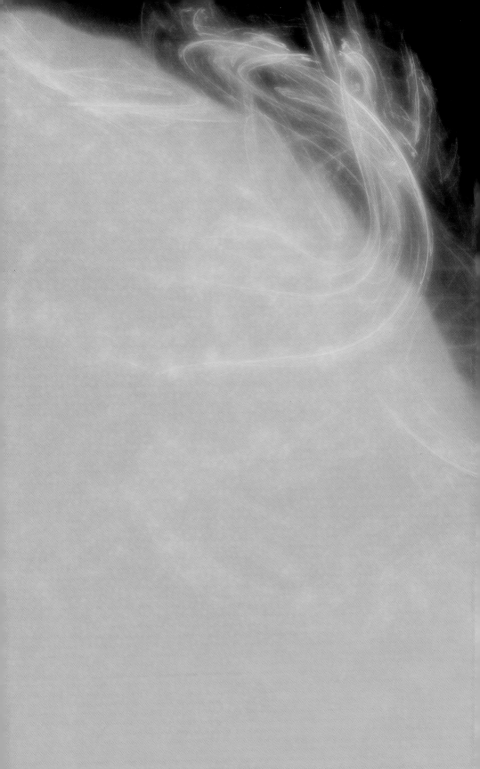

16

The top layer of the sun is called the **corona**, or crown. The corona is much hotter than the photosphere. The temperature of the corona is about 4 million degrees. Sometimes loops of gas from deeper inside the sun push out hundreds of thousands of miles into the corona. Some of these loops travel at 1,300 miles per second! Other loops stay in one place for days or even weeks at a time.

When the sun has a large number of sunspots, there are more **explosions** on its surface. Explosions in the corona release so much energy into space that if we could take that energy, we would never need another source of energy on Earth.

Scientists have discovered that most stars have a corona.

A Star's Life

A star goes through different stages of life. What a star is called depends on how old and how big the star is. As a star gets older, it may be called a red giant, then a white dwarf. This is the last stage of a star's life. The star will then explode and become a **supernova**. This takes billions of years.

At just over 4.5 billion years old, our sun is still young. It has not reached these stages in a star's life yet. As hydrogen is used up in the sun's core, the sun will enter its red giant stage like this star in the photo on the right. When this happens, Earth's temperature will become too hot for life to exist. Scientists believe this will happen around 5 billion years from now.

A star enters its red giant stage as the hydrogen in its core is used up.

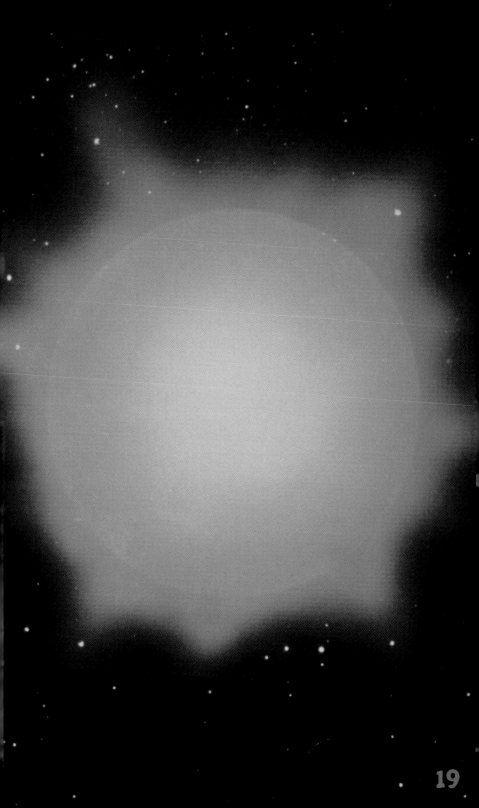

The Sun and You

Take a look around you. The sun gives heat, light, and energy to all living things. The heat and light from the sun allow plants to grow. Plants give animals and people food to eat. The sun also gives energy to trees and makes them grow. Trees give off a gas we need to breathe.

The sun also gives us rain and snow. Heat from the sun causes water on Earth to **evaporate**. This water forms the clouds we see in the sky. Water falls from the clouds as rain or snow and enters the rivers, lakes, and oceans. This is how Earth gets its water. All living things need water to live. Without the sun, there would be no rain or snow.

There would be no rain, snow, trees, flowers, animals, or people without the sun.

The sun is more than just a big ball shining in the sky. It's full of gases and energy. Without the sun, we wouldn't have daylight or plants or animals.

We need the sun for many things, so it is important to respect the sun's power. The sun helps us, but it can also be harmful. It gives off rays that can hurt your skin. Always protect yourself when you are outside in the sun. As long as we remember how powerful the sun is, we can safely enjoy its warmth and beautiful light.

Glossary

astronomer   A person who studies outer space.

axis   A straight, imaginary line on which the sun spins.

corona   The top layer of the sun.

evaporate   To change from a liquid to a vapor.

explosion   The action of blowing up.

galaxy   A large group of stars and the planets that circle them.

helium   A very light gas that will not burn.

hydrogen   A gas that burns easily. It is the lightest gas.

photosphere   The layer of the sun that we can see.

pressure   A force put on something.

solar system   The system made up of our sun, the nine planets, moons, and other space objects.

spiral   A winding coil.

supernova   An exploding star.

temperature   How hot or cold something is.

Index

DATE DUE			